# Playing with Plays™
# Presents
# Jane Austen's

# EMMA

## FOR KIDS
### (The melodramatic version!)

For 6-15 actors, or kids of all ages who want to have fun!
Creatively modified by Amanda Thayer & Brendan P. Kelso
Cover stage illustrated by Shana Hallmeyer
Cover illustrations by Adam Watson,
and Ron Leishman

3 Melodramatic Modifications
for 3 different group sizes:

6-9 actors

9-12 actors

12-15 actors

# Table Of Contents

To Jeanne,
Just because you deserve it!

-BPK

To Jenni who match-maked me with my husband.
And to my husband who always encourages me to write.
-ART

---



For performance rights please see
page 6 of this book or contact:

contact@PlayingWithPlays.com

# Foreword

When I was in high school there was something about Shakespeare that appealed to me. Not that I understood it mind you, but there were clear scenes and images that always stood out in my mind. Romeo & Juliet, "Romeo, Romeo; wherefore art thou Romeo?"; Julius Caesar, "Et tu Brute"; Macbeth, "Double, Double, toil and trouble"; Hamlet, "to be or not to be"; A Midsummer Night's Dream, all I remember about this was a wickedly cool fairy and something about a guy turning into a donkey that I thought was pretty funny. It was not until I started analyzing Shakespeare's plays as an actor that I realized one very important thing, I still didn't understand them. Seriously though, it's tough enough for adults, let alone kids. Then it hit me, why don't I make a version that kids could perform, but make it easy for them to understand with a splash of Shakespeare lingo mixed in? And voila! A melodramatic masterpiece was created! They are intended to be melodramatically fun!

THE PLAYS: There are 3 plays within this book, for three different group sizes. The reason: to allow educators or parents to get the story across to their children regardless of the size of their group. As you read through the plays, there are several lines that are highlighted. These are actual lines from the original book. I am a little more particular about the kids saying these lines verbatim. But the rest, well... have fun!

The entire purpose of this book is to instill the love of a classic story, as well as drama, into the kids.

And when you have children who have a passion for something, they will start to teach themselves, with or without school.

These plays are intended for pure fun. Please DO NOT have the kids learn these lines verbatim, that would be a complete waste of creativity. But do have them basically know their lines and improvise wherever they want as long as it pertains to telling the story. Because that is the goal of an actor: to tell the story. In A Midsummer Night's Dream, I once had a student playing Quince question me about one of her lines, "but in the actual story, didn't the Mechanicals state that 'they would hang us'?" I thought for a second and realized that she had read the story with her mom, and she was right. So I let her add the line she wanted and it added that much more fun, it made the play theirs. I have had kids throw water on the audience, run around the audience, sit in the audience, lose their pumpkin pants (size 30 around a size 15 doesn't work very well, but makes for some great humor!) and most importantly, die all over the stage. The kids love it.

One last note: if you want some educational resources, loved our plays, want to tell the world how much your kids loved performing Shakespeare, want to insult someone with our Shakespeare Insult Generator, or are just a fan of Shakespeare, then hop on our website and have fun:

PlayingWithPlays.com

With these notes, I'll see you on the stage, have fun, and break a leg!

I've been teaching these plays as afterschool and summer programs for quite some time. Many people have asked what the program is, therefore, I have put together a basic formula so any teacher or parent can follow and have melodramatic success! As well, many teachers use my books in a variety of ways. You can view the formula and many more resources on my website at: PlayingWithPlays.com


- Brendan


## OTHER PLAYS AND FULL LENGTH SCRIPTS

We have over 25 different titles, as well as a full-length play in 4-acts for theatre groups: Shakespeare's Hilarious Tragedies. You can see all of our other titles on our website here: PlayingWithPlays.com/books

As well, you can see a sneak peek at some of those titles at the back of this book.

And, if you ever have any questions, please don't hesitate to ask at: Contact@PlayingWithPlays.com

# LICENSES AND ROYALTIES

All performances and other productions require the issuance of a license. Here are the basic guidelines:

1) Please contact us! We always LOVE to hear about a school or group performing our books! We would also love to share photos and brag about your program as well! (with your permission, of course)

2) We require that you purchase a copy of the play for the director/teacher and each kid in the show.

3) If you are a group and DO NOT charge your kids to be in the production, contact us about our educational rates to get a copy in each kid's hands inexpensively. (we will make this work for you!)

4) If you are a group and DO charge your kids to be in the production, (i.e. afterschool program, summer camp), contact us for bulk (10 books or more) or educator's discounts.

5) If you are a group and DO NOT charge the audience to see the plays, please see our website FAQs (www.PlayingWithPlays.com) to see if you are eligible to waive the performance license(s) (most performances are eligible).

6) If you are a group and DO charge the audience to see the performance, please see our website FAQs for performance licensing fees (this includes performances for donations and competitions).

Any other questions or comments, please see our website or email us at:

contact@PlayingWithPlays.com

# The 15-Minute or so
# EMMA
# for Kids

by Jane Austen
Creatively modified by
Amanda Thayer & Brendan P. Kelso
## 6-9 Actors

## CAST OF CHARACTERS:

**EMMA:** Wealthy, "match-maker" extraordinaire!

[1]**MR. WOODHOUSE:** Emma's father

**MR. KNIGHTLEY:** Wealthy; counsels Emma (whether she likes it or not!)

[3]**HARRIET SMITH:** Emma's friend, always falling in love

[1]**MR. ELTON:** Vicar in Highbury

[2]**MRS. WESTON:** Previous governess of Emma (aka Miss Taylor)

[2]**MISS BATES:** Talkative and poor

[3]**JANE FAIRFAX:** Educated and poor. Secret fiancé of Frank Churchill.

**FRANK CHURCHILL:** Son of Mr. Weston, raised by Churchill relatives.

The same actors can play the following parts:
[1]MR. WOODHOUSE and MR. ELTON
[2]MISS BATES and MRS. WESTON
[3]JANE FAIRFAX and HARRIET SMITH

<h1 style="text-align:center">ACT 1 SCENE 1</h1>

*(enter EMMA and MR. WOODHOUSE who is in despair)*

**MR. WOODHOUSE:** Poor Miss Taylor!— I wish she were here again. Emma, getting married is lame and makes everyone sad.

**EMMA:** I cannot agree with you, Papa. And now she has a house of her own!

**MR. WOODHOUSE:** Why would she want her own house?! Our house is three times as large! Downgrade much?

*(enter MR. KNIGHTLEY)*

**MR. KNIGHTLEY:** Congratulations! You must be so excited about Miss Taylor and Mr. Weston getting married.

**MR. WOODHOUSE:** Ugh. No.

**EMMA:** I'm happy. I was their match-maker, which is quite impressive, and you should be impressed.

*(MR. KNIGHTLEY is not impressed)*

**MR. KNIGHTLEY:** You did not. You made a lucky guess and that is all that can be said.

**EMMA:** Same thing! *(sticks tongue out)*

**MR. KNIGHTLEY:** Is not!

**EMMA:** Is too!

**MR. WOODHOUSE:** Please stop flirting. I'm trying to be sad.

*(EMMA and MR. KNIGHTLEY both look in opposite directions and start whistling awkwardly)*

**EMMA:** Sigh. But now I have no friends. No one in town is good enough to be my friend. You are probably my best friend now, Mr. Knightley. How depressing.

**MR. KNIGHTLEY:** Uhhhhhhhh..........

*(enter HARRIET)*

**HARRIET:** Wait! I'll be your best friend! My name is Harriet and I am young, naive, and have no family. You could probably take pity on me.

**EMMA:** I will take pity on you!

*(ALL exit)*

# ACT 1 SCENE 2

*(enter EMMA and HARRIET; enter MR. KNIGHTLEY separately, he tries to blend in with the stage holding a 'bush')*

**EMMA:** Harriet, you are pretty and better than everyone else. Like me. With my help, you can become a real catch.

**HARRIET:** But I think I am already in love with the farmer, Robert Martin. I stayed with his sisters on their farm this summer.

**EMMA:** A farmer?!

**HARRIET:** Yes! Do you know him?

**EMMA:** Scoff. A young farmer, whether on horseback or on foot, is the very last sort of person to raise my curiosity. *(HARRIET looks dismayed)* Uhhhhh...what does he look like?

**HARRIET:** Oh! Not handsome. I thought him very plain at first, but I do not think him so plain now.

**EMMA:** Plain? He sounds... amazing. But you can't be in love with a farmer, especially a plain one. I'm going to set you up with hot Mr. Elton, the Vicar.

**HARRIET:** Yippee! I can't wait to go on a date with hot Mr. Elton.

**EMMA:** Hurray for my match-making powers!

**HARRIET:** What's this? Robert Martin, THE FARMER, is proposing marriage to me. WHAT SHOULD I DO?! Emma, please help me!

**EMMA:** I really shouldn't tell you what to do... buuuut... ditch that guy and let me set you up with Mr. Elton.

**HARRIET:** You mean, HOT Mr. Elton?

**EMMA:** Exactly.

**HARRIET:** Okay, sounds good.

*(HARRIET exits; EMMA does a victory dance)*

**MR. KNIGHTLEY:** Emma!

**EMMA:** *(startled)* Ahhhh!!!

**MR. KNIGHTLEY:** I just heard marvelous news! The farmer, Robert Martin, has proposed to Harriet.

**EMMA:** Mr. Knightley! Were you hiding in that bush??

**MR. KNIGHTLEY:** Uhhh no. Why would I do that? That would be weird.

**EMMA:** Ooooooookayyyy.

*(awkward moment)*

**MR. KNIGHTLEY:** So, hurray for Robert Martin and Harriet!

**EMMA:** What? No, no, no! I just told Harriet to reject him! Isn't that great? Now she can marry a real gentleman! *(to audience)* Like hot Mr. Elton.

**MR. KNIGHTLEY:** Why would you do that?!

**EMMA:** *(sighs)* It is always incomprehensible to a man that a woman should ever refuse an offer of marriage. A man always imagines a woman to be ready for anybody who asks her.

**MR. KNIGHTLEY:** But no one else will ask her! She is the natural daughter of nobody knows whom. She is not a sensible girl and has been taught nothing useful.

**EMMA:** Ouch! She is still better than an ignorant farmer.

**MR. KNIGHTLEY:** Ignorant farmer?? Robert Martin is a respectable, intelligent gentleman-farmer!

*(voice offstage: Yee-haw!)*

**EMMA:** You hear that?! Still a farmer! Ugh... you don't know anything! I think Harriet can do better than plain Robert Martin, so that is what will happen!

*(EMMA sticks tongue out at MR. KNIGHTLEY and exits; MR. KNIGHTLEY slaps hand against forehead and exits opposite)*

*(enter EMMA, HARRIET, and MR. ELTON)*

**EMMA:** Harriet, I would like to introduce you to Mr. Elton. Mr. Elton, this is Harriet. *(to audience)* Let the match-making skills commence!

**HARRIET:** Hello! *(gives subtle thumbs up to EMMA)*

**MR. ELTON:** Hi.

**EMMA:** I know what we should do! Did you ever have your likeness taken, Harriet?

**HARRIET:** Nope!

**MR. ELTON:** You should draw her, Emma! Let me entreat you to exercise so charming a talent in favor of your friend. You draw VERY well.

*(MR. ELTON picks up Emma's portfolio; drawings are all large pictures of stick figures)*

**EMMA:** I can't. I have given up drawing... Okay, you have convinced me! I will do it.

*(EMMA moves to an easel and begins drawing a stick figure of Harriet)*

**MR. ELTON:** Oh, Miss Woodhouse, it is brilliant! It looks just like her!

**EMMA:** Done!

*(EMMA turns the stick-figure picture around to show HARRIET)*

**HARRIET:** Gasp! Do you think it is a true likeness? It is way more beautiful than me. Emma, you are perfect at everything.

**EMMA:** I know.

**MR. ELTON:** I shall rush to London immediately to get it framed.

*(MR. ELTON grabs the picture and runs offstage)*

**EMMA:** He totally loves you.

**HARRIET:** You think?

*(EMMA nods; they exit high-fiving)*

*(enter EMMA and MR. ELTON from one direction; enter MRS. WESTON from opposite with something Christmassy)*

**EMMA:** It is such a bummer that Harriet is sick and couldn't make it to this Christmas party.

**MR. ELTON:** Yes. Poor Miss Smith. But, can I get YOU a drink, Miss Woodhouse? Do you want to hang out with me?

**EMMA:** Oh. Uhhhh. No, thank you.

**MR. ELTON:** What a wonderful dinner party this is! It is certainly a small party, but where small parties are select, they are perhaps the most agreeable of any.

**EMMA:** What?

**MR. ELTON:** It's easier to talk with people.

**EMMA:** Oh, yeah. Speaking of talking, I'm going to go talk to Mrs. Weston.

*(EMMA walks to MRS. WESTON)*

**EMMA:** *(to audience)* Mr. Elton must compose his joyous looks. Harriet seems quite forgotten in the expectation of a pleasant party.

**MRS. WESTON:** Hi, Emma!

**EMMA:** Hi, Mrs. Weston! I hear Frank Churchill, *(to audience)* the son Mr. Weston gave up when he was two, *(to Mrs. Weston)* is finally coming to visit.

**MRS. WESTON:** *(sighs)* I don't think he will really come.

**EMMA:** Yeah. Frank's grumpy aunt never lets him do anything. Hopefully, it works out!

**MRS. WESTON:** Hopefully! Also, I'm sorry Miss Smith is sick.

**EMMA:** I KNOW. Poor Harriet.

*(MR. ELTON pops out from behind EMMA and MRS. WESTON where he has been lurking)*

**MR. ELTON:** Poor Miss Smith! But, Mrs. Weston, you must promise to help me persuade Emma, I mean, Miss Woodhouse, to stop visiting Miss Smith while she is sick. Miss Woodhouse is so scrupulous for others and yet so careless for herself. Is that fair, Mrs. Weston?

**MRS. WESTON:** Uhhh... Oh look, it's snowing outside! I must leave now or I will die in the snow!

*(MRS. WESTON exits)*

**MR. ELTON:** Miss Woodhouse, I love you!

**EMMA:** Say whhhhaaaaattt??

**MR. ELTON:** Everything that I have said or done, for many weeks past, has been with the sole view of marking my admiration of yourself. I am sure you have seen and understood me.

**EMMA:** So you're saying you're not in love with Miss Smith? You know... Harriet?

**MR. ELTON:** Miss Smith?! I never thought of Miss Smith in the whole course of my existence. Who can think of Miss Smith when Miss Woodhouse is near?

**EMMA**: Very Shakespeare of you. Well, this stinks.

**MR. ELTON**: Stinks? That's a curious way to say you love me too.

**EMMA**: Ummm, yeah... not going to happen.

**MR. ELTON**: What?

**EMMA**: Let me see, how can I put this simply? .... I don't love you?

**MR. ELTON**: Ugh! Love? Fine then! Bye!

**EMMA**: Sorry. Geez. Bye.

*(ALL exit)*

*(enter EMMA, pacing)*

**EMMA:** Well, I messed up big time. I actually talked poor Harriet into being very much attached to this man. It was foolish, it was wrong, to take so active a part in bringing any two people together. I resolve to do such things no more.

*(EMMA sighs loudly; enter HARRIET)*

**HARRIET:** Hi! How was the party?

**EMMA:** This is awkward. Mr. Elton loves me. Not you.

*(HARRIET'S jaw drops, long silence)*

**EMMA:** Harriet, are you okay??

**HARRIET:** Obviously, I'm not good enough for him. I am sad.

*(HARRIET frowns exaggeratedly)*

**EMMA:** I will distract you with fun activities, so you don't think about him!

**HARRIET:** Should I think about the farmer?

**EMMA:** No.

**HARRIET:** Alright. Fun activities. That's fine I guess.

*(ALL exit)*

## ACT 2 SCENE 2

*(enter EMMA and HARRIET)*

**EMMA**: Harriet, let's visit Miss Bates. Miss Bates talks a LOT and is TOTALLY annoying, but it is our duty to be nice to her since she is poor.

*(EMMA and HARRIET walk around stage; enter MISS BATES)*

**MISS BATES**: Hello! It is so nice of you to come for a visit.

**EMMA**: Thank you for having us.

**MISS BATES**: Even though we are poor.

**EMMA**: Of course.

**MISS BATES**: So poor.

**EMMA**: Ahhh...

**MISS BATES**: Oh! Have I ever told you about my orphaned but well-educated niece, Jane Fairfax?

**EMMA**: Only literally every time I see you.

**MISS BATES**: She was raised by the Campbells' but now must forsake good society to become a governess.

**EMMA**: Oh.

**MISS BATES**: So sad.

**HARRIET**: Yes. So sad.

**MISS BATES:** Well, I received a letter stating she is coming to visit next week! Jane caught a bad cold last November. Her kind friends the Campbells think she had better come home and try an air that always agrees with her. Now I will read you her letter.

**EMMA:** *(to HARRIET)* Will this visit ever end?? *(to MISS BATES)* How wonderful for you that Jane is coming! But, I am afraid we must be running away. My father will be expecting us. Soooo... bye!

**MISS BATES:** But the letter...

**EMMA:** Next time!

*(EMMA grabs HARRIET'S hand and they rush off stage; MISS BATES exits opposite)*

**ACT 2 SCENE 3**

*(enter EMMA opposite MISS BATES with JANE hiding behind)*

**MISS BATES:** Mr. Elton is getting married!

**EMMA:** Didn't I just see you??

**MISS BATES:** No. That was the other day. Plus, didn't you notice Jane is with me?

*(JANE sheepishly steps out from behind MISS BATES, eyes wide, staring at the floor)*

**EMMA:** Oh, hey, Jane. You look... tired?

**JANE:** Yes.

**MISS BATES:** Run along, Jane. Get some rest.

*(JANE quickly exits)*

**EMMA:** So. Wait. WHAT?! Who is Mr. Elton marrying?!

**MISS BATES:** A Miss Hawkins—that's all I know. A Miss Hawkins of Bath.

**EMMA:** Well, that was fast.

**MISS BATES:** Yes. But how exciting! Also, thank you for giving me that ham since I am poor. Bye!

*(MISS BATES exits)*

**EMMA:** Ugh! Now I have to tell Harriet that Mr. Elton is engaged!

*(enter HARRIET)*

**EMMA**: *(to audience)* Let's get this over with. *(to HARRIET)* Mr. Elton is engaged!

**HARRIET**: Well that stinks! But guess what? I ran into Mr. Martin.

**EMMA**: The farmer? But...

**HARRIET**: *(continues over EMMA)* We talked and there was a sort of satisfaction in seeing him behave so pleasantly and so kindly. I think he might still be in love with me! *(to audience)* And I think I might still be in love with him!

**EMMA**: No more Robert Martin!

**HARRIET**: Whoops. Sorry. Please find someone else for me to love.

**EMMA**: On it.

*(ALL exit)*

*(Enter FRANK, MRS. WESTON, and MR. KNIGHTLEY; enter EMMA opposite)*

**EMMA:** *(to audience)* We are at a dinner party at the Cole's. I'm better than them, but I came because my friends are here. Also, Frank Churchill finally came for a visit.

*(EMMA points to FRANK; he waves)*

**EMMA:** *(to FRANK)* Did you hear that Jane was sent a piano by a secret admirer?

**FRANK:** Oh REALLY?? I wonder who that could be from. *(winks at audience)*

**MRS. WESTON:** Pssst, Emma! Come here!

*(EMMA crosses to MRS. WESTON)*

**EMMA:** What's up?

**MRS. WESTON:** Did you know Mr. Knightley sent his own carriage to pick up Miss Bates and Jane Fairfax for the party tonight? I think he is the one who secretly sent her the piano!

**EMMA:** Well... he does like to do any thing really good-natured, useful, considerate, or benevolent.

**MRS. WESTON:** Now, I'm no expert at match-making like you, but what do you think of Mr. Knightley and Miss Fairfax being together?

**EMMA:** Mr. Knightley and Jane Fairfax! The imprudence of such a match. My dear Mrs. Weston, do not take to match-making. You do it very ill.

**MRS. WESTON:** I'm just saying. It could happen.

**EMMA:** Hmph! *(ALL exit)*

*(enter EMMA, FRANK, and MRS. WESTON)*

**FRANK:** That dinner party was fun! We should throw our own ball!

**EMMA, MRS. WESTON:** Yay!

*(letter flies on stage for FRANK)*

**FRANK:** *(opens and reads letter)* Shoot! I have to go back home and help my grumpy aunt! She is "sick" again. The ball must be postponed!

**EMMA, MRS. WESTON:** Boooooooooo.

*(ALL exit except EMMA and FRANK)*

**FRANK:** See ya later, Emma! *(winks at her; exits)*

**EMMA:** Oh no! I think Frank Churchill might be in love with me! And worse, I think I might be in love with him!

*(EMMA paces around the room)*

**EMMA:** But I have sworn I will never get married! When he comes again, if his affection continue, I must be on my guard not to encourage it. *(EMMA sticks finger up like she has had an idea)* Maybe I can set Frank up with Harriet!

*(exits)*

# ACT 4 SCENE 1

*(enter EMMA, FRANK, MRS. WESTON, MR. KNIGHTLEY, HARRIET, and MR. ELTON; ALL spread out and talk in pairs)*

**EMMA:** *(to audience)* I have sworn to not let Frank fall in love with me, but I'm going to keep flirting with him. Because, well... it's fun!

**FRANK:** Will you dance with me? If you don't I might have to dance with Miss Fairfax. Ugh. *(winks at audience)*

**EMMA:** Of course! Everyone thinks we should dance together anyways!

*(EMMA and FRANK start to dance)*

**MR. ELTON:** Mrs. Weston, will you dance with me?

**MRS. WESTON:** No— I am no dancer. You should ask Harriet Smith!

**MR. ELTON:** *(cough-cough)* Uhhh... my dancing days are over, Mrs. Weston. You will excuse me.

*(HARRIET hears and is sad; MR. ELTON walks to talk to someone else; MR. KNIGHTLEY glares at him)*

**EMMA:** *(to MR. KNIGHTLEY)* What's with the evil eye?

**MR. KNIGHTLEY:** Watch this. *(crosses to HARRIET)* Miss Smith, will you dance with me?

**HARRIET:** Oh my goodness! Yes!

*(starts to dance; dance ends)*

**EMMA:** Mr. Knightley, thank you for dancing with Harriet.

**MR. KNIGHTLEY:** Mr. Elton stinks. Will you dance with me now?

**EMMA:** Indeed I will. You have shown that you can dance, and you know we are not really so much brother and sister as to make it at all improper.

*(EMMA and MR. KNIGHTLEY both wink at audience)*

*(ALL exit)*

*(enter EMMA and HARRIET)*

**HARRIET:** I am officially no longer in love with Mr. Elton. However, my life is still sad because now I am in love with someone infinitely better than him.

**EMMA:** I think I know who! *(to audience)* Frank Churchill. *(to Harriet)* The service he rendered you was enough to warm your heart. *(to audience)* He saved her from thieving gypsies.

**HARRIET:** Right?!

**EMMA:** But don't get carried away until you know whether he likes you back.

**HARRIET:** You always give the best advice.

**EMMA:** I know.

*(ALL exit)*

*(enter EMMA, FRANK, MISS BATES, JANE, MR. KNIGHTLEY, HARRIET, and MR. ELTON; ALL spread out and talk in pairs)*

**EMMA:** Ugh. This outing to Box Hill is a drag.

**FRANK:** I have an idea.

*(FRANK claps his hands three times)*

**FRANK:** Attention, everyone! Miss Woodhouse has asked me to lead a game where you all tell her clever things to impress her. Each of you must say one thing very clever, two things moderately clever, or three things very dull indeed.

**MISS BATES:** Oh! Very well, then I need not be uneasy. 'Three things very dull indeed.'

**EMMA:** *(laughing)* Yeah, but you can only say THREE things.

**MISS BATES:** *(frowning)* Ah! Yes, I see what she means. I talk too much. I must make myself very disagreeable. I am obviously a terrible person and no one should be my friend.

**JANE:** Let's go for a walk, Miss Bates.

**MISS BATES:** Yes. Good idea.

*(JANE and MISS BATES exit)*

**MR. KNIGHTLEY:** Emma! *(pause for ALL to awkwardly exit except MR. KNIGHTLEY and EMMA)* How could you be so unfeeling to Miss Bates? Did you forget that she is POOR?? We have to be nice to her! Poorly done, Emma... poorly done.

*(MR. KNIGHTLEY storms off stage)*

**EMMA:** *(to audience)* What is wrong with me? Why do I always think I am better than everyone? Mr. Knightley is always trying to help me be a better person, but I keep failing! I'll go to Miss Bates' house in the morning and apologize.

*(ALL exit)*

*(enter EMMA and MRS. WESTON)*

**MRS. WESTON:** Hey! Before you hang out with Harriet, you should know that Frank Churchill and Jane Fairfax have been secretly engaged for a long time. Also, Frank's grumpy aunt died which means he can finally marry Jane. Okay, bye!

*(MRS. WESTON exits)*

**EMMA:** Oh great. Now I have to tell Harriet that I failed at match-making AGAIN.

*(HARRIET enters)*

**HARRIET:** Hey! What's up!

**EMMA:** Frank Churchill and Jane Fairfax are engaged.

**HARRIET:** Oh yeah! I just heard. I was backstage eavesdropping.

**EMMA:** And... you don't care?

**HARRIET:** Scoff. You do not think I care about Mr. Frank Churchill?

**EMMA:** Yeah huh! You basically told me you are in love with him.

**HARRIET:** No I didn't. I told you I am in love with Mr. Knightley!

**EMMA:** MR. KNIGHTLEY?!

**HARRIET:** I thought you knew. I talked about the great service he rendered me!

**EMMA:** I thought you meant the great service of Frank Churchill protecting you from the gypsies!

**HARRIET:** Oh yeah, that. No, I meant Mr. Knightley's coming and asking me to dance, when Mr. Elton would not stand up with me.

**EMMA:** Oh no. This is not good. *(to audience)* Because I just realized that I love Mr. Knightley.

**HARRIET:** This is awkward... I'm going to go look for a farmer. K bye!

*(ALL exit)*

*(enter EMMA; MR. KNIGHTLEY inconspicuously hiding behind a 'bush')*

**EMMA:** Harriet can't be in love with Mr. Knightley! Mr. Knightley must marry no one but myself!

*(MR. KNIGHTLEY pops out of a bush)*

**MR. KNIGHTLEY:** Emma!

**EMMA:** Ahhh! Why are you always hiding in bushes??

**MR. KNIGHTLEY:** The element of surprise. I love you! *(EMMA'S jaw drops)* Yes, you see, you understand my feelings.

**EMMA:** Duh! Because I love you too!

**MR. KNIGHTLEY:** High five!

*(MR. KNIGHTLEY and EMMA jump and high five)*

**MR. KNIGHTLEY:** I almost forgot! Robert Martin and Harriet are engaged!

**EMMA:** Say whaaaaaaat?

*(enter HARRIET)*

**HARRIET:** We are! YEEHAW!

**MR. KNIGHTLEY:** Yeah, sorry. I know you didn't want them to end up together.

**EMMA:** No, this is great! Especially because I failed every time I tried to set her up with someone!

**HARRIET:** Yes you did!

**MR. KNIGHTLEY:** Awesome! Well, let's all get married then!

**ALL:** Yes!

**THE END**

# The 20-Minute or so
# EMMA
# for Kids
by Jane Austen
Creatively modified by
Amanda Thayer & Brendan P. Kelso
## 9-12 Actors

## CAST OF CHARACTERS:

**EMMA:** Wealthy, "match-maker" extraordinaire!

[1]**MR. WOODHOUSE:** Emma's father

**MR. KNIGHTLEY:** Wealthy; counsels Emma (whether she likes it or not!)

[2]**HARRIET SMITH:** Emma's friend, always falling in love

[3]**MR. ELTON:** Vicar in Highbury

**MRS. WESTON:** Previous governess of Emma (aka Miss Taylor)

**MISS BATES:** Talkative, poor aunt of Jane Fairfax

[1]**ROBERT MARTIN:** Farmer, totally in love with Harriet

[2]**JANE FAIRFAX:** Educated and poor. Secret fiancé of Frank Churchill.

**FRANK CHURCHILL:** Son of Mrs. Weston, raised by Churchill relatives.

**MRS. ELTON:** The new wife of Mr. Elton

[3]**SERVANT:** a servant

The same actors can play the following parts:
[1]MR. WOODHOUSE and ROBERT MARTIN
[2]HARRIET SMITH and JANE FAIRFAX
[3]MR. ELTON and SERVANT

## ACT 1 SCENE 1

*(enter EMMA and MR. WOODHOUSE who is in despair)*

**MR. WOODHOUSE:** Poor Miss Taylor!— I wish she were here again. Emma, getting married is lame and makes everyone sad.

**EMMA:** I cannot agree with you, Papa. And now she has a house of her own!

**MR. WOODHOUSE:** Why would she want her own house?! Our house is three times as large! Downgrade much?

*(enter MR. KNIGHTLEY)*

**MR. KNIGHTLEY:** Congratulations! You must be so excited about Miss Taylor and Mr. Weston getting married.

**MR. WOODHOUSE:** Ugh. No.

**EMMA:** I'm happy. I was their match-maker, which is quite impressive, and you should be impressed.

*(MR. KNIGHTLEY is not impressed)*

**MR. KNIGHTLEY:** You did not. You made a lucky guess and that is all that can be said.

**EMMA:** Same thing! *(sticks tongue out)*

**MR. KNIGHTLEY:** Is not!

**EMMA:** Is too!

**MR. WOODHOUSE:** Please stop flirting. I'm trying to be sad.

*(EMMA and MR. KNIGHTLEY both look in opposite directions and start whistling awkwardly)*

**EMMA:** Sigh. But now I have no friends. No one in town is good enough to be my friend. You are probably my best friend now, Mr. Knightley. How depressing.

**MR. KNIGHTLEY:** Uhhhhhhhh..........

*(enter HARRIET)*

**HARRIET:** Wait! I'll be your best friend! My name is Harriet and I am young, naive, and have no family. You could probably take pity on me.

**EMMA:** I will take pity on you!

*(ALL exit)*

ACT 1 SCENE 2

*(enter EMMA and HARRIET; enter MR. KNIGHTLEY separately, he tries to blend in with the stage holding a 'bush')*

**EMMA:** Harriet, you are pretty and better than everyone else. Like me. With my help, you can become a real catch.

**HARRIET:** But I think I am already in love with the farmer, Robert Martin. I stayed with his sisters on their farm this summer.

**EMMA:** A farmer?!

**HARRIET:** Yes! Do you know him?

**EMMA:** Scoff. A young farmer, whether on horseback or on foot, is the very last sort of person to raise my curiosity. *(HARRIET looks dismayed)* Uhhhhh...what does he look like?

**HARRIET:** Oh! Not handsome. I thought him very plain at first, but I do not think him so plain now.

**EMMA:** Plain? He sounds... amazing. But you can't be in love with a farmer, especially a plain one. I'm going to set you up with hot Mr. Elton, the Vicar.

**HARRIET:** Yippee! I can't wait to go on a date with hot Mr. Elton.

**EMMA:** Hurray for my match-making powers!

*(enter ROBERT)*

**ROBERT:** Well howdy Harriet, I think you should marry me.

**HARRIET:** Ummm... hold that thought for a moment. *(turns to EMMA)* Robert Martin, THE FARMER, is proposing marriage to me. WHAT SHOULD I DO?! Emma, please help me!

**EMMA:** I really shouldn't tell you what to do... buuuut... ditch that guy and let me set you up with Mr. Elton.

**HARRIET:** You mean, HOT Mr. Elton?

**EMMA:** Exactly.

**HARRIET:** Okay, sounds good. *(turns back to ROBERT)* Mr. Martin, we need to talk.

*(they exit; EMMA does a victory dance)*

**MR. KNIGHTLEY:** Emma!

**EMMA:** *(startled)* Ahhhh!!!

**MR. KNIGHTLEY:** I just heard marvelous news! The farmer, Robert Martin, has proposed to Harriet.

**EMMA:** Mr. Knightley! Were you hiding in that bush??

**MR. KNIGHTLEY:** Uhhh no. Why would I do that? That would be weird.

**EMMA:** Ooooooookayyyy.

*(awkward moment)*

**MR. KNIGHTLEY:** So, hurray for Robert Martin and Harriet!

**EMMA:** What? No, no, no! I just told Harriet to reject him! Isn't that great? Now she can marry a real gentleman! *(to audience)* Like hot Mr. Elton.

**MR. KNIGHTLEY:** Why would you do that?!

**EMMA:** *(sighs)* It is always incomprehensible to a man that a woman should ever refuse an offer of marriage. A man always imagines a woman to be ready for anybody who asks her.

**MR. KNIGHTLEY:** But no one else will ask her! She is the natural daughter of nobody knows whom. She is not a sensible girl and has been taught nothing useful.

**EMMA:** Ouch! She is still better than an ignorant farmer.

**MR. KNIGHTLEY:** Ignorant farmer?? Robert Martin is a respectable, intelligent gentleman-farmer!

**ROBERT:** *(offstage)* Yee-haw!

**EMMA:** You hear that?! Still a farmer! Ugh...you don't know anything! I think Harriet can do better than plain Robert Martin, so that is what will happen!

*(EMMA sticks tongue out at MR. KNIGHTLEY and exits; MR. KNIGHTLEY slaps hand against forehead and exits opposite)*

*(enter EMMA, HARRIET, and MR. ELTON)*

**EMMA:** Harriet, I would like to introduce you to Mr. Elton. Mr. Elton, this is Harriet. *(to audience)* Let the match-making skills commence!

**HARRIET:** Hello! *(gives subtle thumbs up to EMMA)*

**MR. ELTON:** Hi.

**EMMA:** I know what we should do! Did you ever have your likeness taken, Harriet?

**HARRIET:** Nope!

**MR. ELTON:** You should draw her, Emma! Let me entreat you to exercise so charming a talent in favor of your friend. You draw VERY well.

*(MR. ELTON picks up Emma's portfolio; drawings are all large pictures of stick figures)*

**EMMA:** I can't. I have given up drawing... Okay, you have convinced me! I will do it.

*(EMMA moves to an easel and begins drawing a stick figure of Harriet)*

**MR. ELTON:** Oh, Miss Woodhouse, it is brilliant! It looks just like her!

**EMMA:** Done!

*(EMMA turns the stick-figure picture around to show HARRIET)*

**HARRIET:** Gasp! Do you think it is a true likeness? It is way more beautiful than me. Emma, you are perfect at everything.

**EMMA:** I know.

**MR. ELTON:** I shall rush to London immediately to get it framed.

*(MR. ELTON grabs the picture and runs offstage)*

**EMMA:** He totally loves you.

**HARRIET:** You think?

*(EMMA nods; they exit high-fiving)*

## ACT 1 SCENE 4

*(enter EMMA and MR. ELTON from one direction; enter MRS. WESTON, and MR. WOODHOUSE from opposite)*

**EMMA:** It is such a bummer that Harriet is sick and couldn't make it to this Christmas party.

**MR. ELTON:** Yes. Poor Miss Smith. But, can I get YOU a drink, Miss Woodhouse? Do you want to hang out with me?

**EMMA:** Oh. Uhhhh. No, thank you.

**MR. ELTON:** What a wonderful dinner party this is! It is certainly a small party, but where small parties are select, they are perhaps the most agreeable of any.

**EMMA:** What?

**MR. ELTON:** It's easier to talk with people.

**EMMA:** Oh, yeah. Speaking of talking, I'm going to go talk to Mrs. Weston.

*(EMMA walks to MRS. WESTON)*

**EMMA:** *(to audience)* Mr. Elton must compose his joyous looks. Harriet seems quite forgotten in the expectation of a pleasant party.

**MRS. WESTON:** Hi, Emma!

**EMMA:** Hi, Mrs. Weston! I hear Frank Churchill, *(to audience)* the son Mr. Weston gave up when he was two, *(to Mrs. Weston)* is finally coming to visit.

**MRS. WESTON:** *(sighs)* I don't think he will really come.

**EMMA:** Yeah. Frank's grumpy aunt never lets him do anything. Hopefully, it works out!

**MRS. WESTON:** Hopefully! Also, I'm sorry Miss Smith is sick.

**EMMA:** I KNOW. Poor Harriet.

*(MR. ELTON pops out from behind EMMA and MRS. WESTON where he has been lurking)*

**MR. ELTON:** Poor Miss Smith! But, Mrs. Weston, you must promise to help me persuade Emma, I mean, Miss Woodhouse, to stop visiting Miss Smith while she is sick. Miss Woodhouse is so scrupulous for others and yet so careless for herself. Is that fair, Mrs. Weston?

**MRS. WESTON:** Uh...

**MR. WOODHOUSE:** *(to audience)* Oh-no! Diversion needed... Ummm... Oh look, it's snowing outside! We must leave now or we will all die in the snow!

*(ALL exit except EMMA and MR. ELTON)*

**MR. ELTON:** Miss Woodhouse, I love you!

**EMMA:** Say whhhhaaaaattt??

**MR. ELTON:** Everything that I have said or done, for many weeks past, has been with the sole view of marking my admiration of yourself. I am sure you have seen and understood me.

**EMMA:** So you're saying you're not in love with Miss Smith? You know... Harriet?

**MR. ELTON:** Miss Smith?! I never thought of Miss Smith in the whole course of my existence. Who can think of Miss Smith when Miss Woodhouse is near?

**EMMA:** Very Shakespeare of you. Well, this stinks.

**MR. ELTON:** Stinks? That's a curious way to say you love me too.

**EMMA:** Ummm, yeah... not going to happen.

**MR. ELTON:** What?

**EMMA:** Let me see, how can I put this simply? .... I don't love you?

**MR. ELTON:** Ugh! Love? Fine then! Bye!

**EMMA:** Sorry. Geez. Bye.

*(ALL exit)*

*(enter EMMA, pacing)*

**EMMA:** Well, I messed up big time. I actually talked poor Harriet into being very much attached to this man. It was foolish, it was wrong, to take so active a part in bringing any two people together. I resolve to do such things no more.

*(EMMA sighs loudly; enter HARRIET)*

**HARRIET:** Hi! How was the party?

**EMMA:** This is awkward. Mr. Elton loves me. Not you.

*(HARRIET'S jaw drops, long silence)*

**EMMA:** Harriet, are you okay??

**HARRIET:** Obviously, I'm not good enough for him. I am sad.

*(HARRIET frowns exaggeratedly)*

**EMMA:** I will distract you with fun activities, so you don't think about him!

**HARRIET:** Should I think about the farmer?

**EMMA:** No.

**HARRIET:** Alright. Fun activities. That's fine I guess.

*(ALL exit)*

*(enter EMMA and HARRIET)*

**EMMA**: Harriet, let's visit Miss Bates. Miss Bates talks a LOT and is TOTALLY annoying, but it is our duty to be nice to her since she is poor.

*(EMMA and HARRIET walk around stage; enter MISS BATES)*

**MISS BATES**: Hello! It is so nice of you to come for a visit.

**EMMA**: Thank you for having us.

**MISS BATES**: Even though we are poor.

**EMMA**: Of course.

**MISS BATES**: So poor.

**EMMA**: Ahhh...

**MISS BATES**: Oh! Have I ever told you about my orphaned but well-educated niece, Jane Fairfax?

**EMMA**: Only literally every time I see you.

**MISS BATES**: She was raised by the Campbells' but now must forsake good society to become a governess.

**EMMA**: Oh.

**MISS BATES**: So sad.

**HARRIET**: Yes. So sad.

**MISS BATES:** Well, I received a letter stating she is coming to visit next week! Jane caught a bad cold last November. Her kind friends the Campbells think she had better come home and try an air that always agrees with her. Now I will read you her letter.

**EMMA:** *(to HARRIET)* Will this visit ever end?? *(to MISS BATES)* How wonderful for you that Jane is coming! But, I am afraid we must be running away. My father will be expecting us. Soooo... bye!

**MISS BATES:** But the letter...

**EMMA:** Next time!

*(EMMA grabs HARRIET'S hand and they rush off stage; MISS BATES exits opposite)*

*(enter EMMA opposite MISS BATES with JANE hiding behind)*

**MISS BATES:** Mr. Elton is getting married!

**EMMA:** Didn't I just see you??

**MISS BATES:** No. That was the other day. Plus, didn't you notice Jane is with me?

*(JANE sheepishly steps out from behind MISS BATES, eyes wide, staring at the floor)*

**EMMA:** Oh, hey, Jane. You look... tired?

*(JANE nods her head)*

**EMMA:** So. Wait. WHAT?! Who is Mr. Elton marrying?!

**MISS BATES:** A Miss Hawkins—that's all I know. A Miss Hawkins of Bath.

**EMMA:** Well, that was fast.

**MISS BATES:** Yes. But how exciting! Also, thank you for giving me that ham since I am poor. Bye!

*(MISS BATES exits; JANE quickly follows)*

**EMMA:** Ugh! Now I have to tell Harriet that Mr. Elton is engaged!

*(enter HARRIET)*

**EMMA:** *(to audience)* Let's get this over with. *(to HARRIET)* Mr. Elton is engaged!

**HARRIET:** Well that stinks! But guess what? I ran into Mr. Martin.

**EMMA:** The farmer? But...

**HARRIET:** *(continues over EMMA)* We talked and there was a sort of satisfaction in seeing him behave so pleasantly and so kindly. I think he might still be in love with me! *(to audience)* And I think I might still be in love with him!

**EMMA:** No more Robert Martin!

**HARRIET:** Whoops. Sorry. Please find someone else for me to love.

**EMMA:** On it.

*(ALL exit)*

<h1 style="text-align:center">ACT 3 SCENE 1</h1>

*(Enter FRANK, MRS. WESTON, MISS BATES, JANE, and MR. KNIGHTLEY; ALL spread out and talk in pairs; enter EMMA)*

**EMMA:** *(to audience)* We are at a dinner party at the Cole's. I'm better than them, but I came because my friends are here. Also, Frank Churchill finally came for a visit.

*(EMMA points to FRANK; he waves)*

**EMMA:** *(to FRANK)* Did you hear that Jane was sent a piano by a secret admirer?

**FRANK:** Oh REALLY?? I wonder who that could be from. *(winks at audience)*

**MRS. WESTON:** Pssst, Emma! Come here!

*(EMMA crosses to MRS. WESTON)*

**EMMA:** What's up?

**MRS. WESTON:** Did you know Mr. Knightley sent his own carriage to pick up Miss Bates and Jane Fairfax for the party tonight? I think he is the one who secretly sent her the piano!

**EMMA:** Well... he does like to do any thing really good-natured, useful, considerate, or benevolent.

**MRS. WESTON:** Now, I'm no expert at match-making like you, but what do you think of Mr. Knightley and Miss Fairfax being together?

**EMMA:** Mr. Knightley and Jane Fairfax! The imprudence of such a match. My dear Mrs. Weston, do not take to match-making. You do it very ill.

**MRS. WESTON:** I'm just saying. It could happen.

**EMMA:** Hmph! *(ALL exit)*

*(enter EMMA, FRANK, MRS. WESTON, and MISS BATES)*

**FRANK:** That dinner party was fun! We should throw our own ball!

**EMMA, MRS. WESTON, MISS BATES:** Yay!

*(SERVANT enters with a letter for FRANK)*

**FRANK:** *(opens and reads letter)* Shoot! I have to go back home and help my grumpy aunt! She is "sick" again. The ball must be postponed!

**EMMA, MRS. WESTON, MISS BATES:** Boooooooooo.

*(ALL exit except EMMA and FRANK)*

**FRANK:** See ya later, Emma! *(winks at her; exits)*

**EMMA:** Oh no! I think Frank Churchill might be in love with me! And worse, I think I might be in love with him!

*(EMMA paces around the room)*

**EMMA:** But I have sworn I will never get married! When he comes again, if his affection continue, I must be on my guard not to encourage it. *(EMMA sticks finger up like she has had an idea)* Maybe I can set Frank up with Harriet!

*(exits)*

*(enter EMMA, MRS. ELTON, MRS. WESTON, MISS BATES, JANE, and MR. KNIGHTLEY)*

**EMMA:** *(to audience)* The new Mrs. Elton has finally arrived. She is SUPER fancy and SUPER full of herself, but I have to throw her a dinner party to welcome her to our beautiful little town.

**MRS. ELTON:** What do you think of that poor Jane Fairfax? Can you believe she has to become a GOVERNESS?! That is, like, the worst job EVER!

**MRS. WESTON:** Cough! I'm standing right here!

**EMMA:** Mrs. Weston was my governess.

**MRS. ELTON:** Whoops. Sorry. Anyways, I am going to force Jane to be my friend and then I will find her a governess job in a big fancy house.

**EMMA:** That's nice of you... I guess.

**MRS. ELTON:** It is, isn't it? Hey! Miss Fairfax! Over here!

**JANE:** Hello.

**MRS. ELTON:** Jane, I am going to find you the perfect governess job. You have not seen so much of the world as I have. We must begin inquiring directly.

**JANE:** Excuse me, ma'am, but this is by no means my intention; I make no inquiry myself, and should be sorry to have any made by my friends.

**MRS. ELTON:** Fine. But I am going to keep bugging you about it!

*(enter SERVANT, hands a letter to MRS. WESTON)*

**MRS. WESTON:** *(reads letter)* Hurray! Frank is coming to visit again! *(ALL exit)*

# ACT 4 SCENE 1

*(enter EMMA, FRANK, MRS. WESTON, MISS BATES, MR. KNIGHTLEY, HARRIET, MR. ELTON, and MRS. ELTON. ALL spread out and talk in pairs)*

**EMMA:** *(to audience)* I have sworn to not let Frank fall in love with me, but I'm going to keep flirting with him. Because, well... it's fun!

**FRANK:** Will you dance with me? If you don't I might have to dance with Miss Fairfax. Ugh. *(winks at audience)*

**EMMA:** Of course! Everyone thinks we should dance together anyways!

*(EMMA and FRANK start to dance)*

**MR. ELTON:** Mrs. Weston, will you dance with me?

**MRS. WESTON:** No— I am no dancer. You should ask Harriet Smith!

**MR. ELTON:** *(cough-cough)* Uhhh... my dancing days are over, Mrs. Weston. You will excuse me.

*((HARRIET hears and is sad; MR. ELTON walks to talk to someone else; MR. KNIGHTLEY glares at him)*

**EMMA:** *(to MR. KNIGHTLEY)* What's with the evil eye?

**MR. KNIGHTLEY:** Watch this. *(crosses to HARRIET)* Miss Smith, will you dance with me?

**HARRIET:** Oh my goodness! Yes!

*(starts to dance; dance ends)*

**EMMA**: Mr. Knightley, thank you for dancing with Harriet.

**MR. KNIGHTLEY**: Mr. Elton stinks. Will you dance with me now?

**EMMA**: Indeed I will. You have shown that you can dance, and you know we are not really so much brother and sister as to make it at all improper.

*(EMMA and MR. KNIGHTLEY both wink at audience)*

*(ALL exit)*

# ACT 4 SCENE 2

*(enter EMMA and HARRIET)*

**HARRIET:** I am officially no longer in love with Mr. Elton. However, my life is still sad because now I am in love with someone infinitely better than him.

**EMMA:** I think I know who! *(to audience)* Frank Churchill. *(to Harriet)* The service he rendered you was enough to warm your heart. *(to audience)* He saved her from thieving gypsies.

**HARRIET:** Right?!

**EMMA:** But don't get carried away until you know whether he likes you back.

**HARRIET:** You always give the best advice.

**EMMA:** I know.

*(ALL exit)*

*(enter EMMA, FRANK, MRS. WESTON, MISS BATES, JANE, MR. KNIGHTLEY, MR. ELTON, and MRS. ELTON; ALL spread out and talk in pairs)*

**EMMA:** Ugh. This outing to Box Hill is a drag.

**FRANK:** I have an idea.

*(FRANK claps his hands three times)*

**FRANK:** Attention, everyone! Miss Woodhouse has asked me to lead a game where you all tell her clever things to impress her. Each of you must say one thing very clever, two things moderately clever, or three things very dull indeed.

**MISS BATES:** Oh! Very well, then I need not be uneasy. 'Three things very dull indeed.'

**EMMA:** *(laughing)* Yeah, but you can only say THREE things.

**MISS BATES:** *(frowning)* Ah! Yes, I see what she means. I talk too much. I must make myself very disagreeable. I am obviously a terrible person and no one should be my friend.

**JANE:** Let's go for a walk with Mrs. Elton.

**MISS BATES:** Yes. Good idea.

*(JANE, MRS. ELTON, and MISS BATES exit)*

**MR. KNIGHTLEY:** Emma! *(pause for ALL to awkwardly exit except MR. KNIGHTLEY and EMMA)* How could you be so unfeeling to Miss Bates? Did you forget that she is POOR?? We have to be nice to her! Poorly done, Emma... poorly done.

*(MR. KNIGHTLEY storms off stage)*

**EMMA:** *(to audience)* What is wrong with me? Why do I always think I am better than everyone? Mr. Knightley is always trying to help me be a better person, but I keep failing! I'll go to Miss Bates' house in the morning and apologize.

*(ALL exit)*

# ACT 4 SCENE 4

*(enter EMMA and MRS. WESTON)*

**MRS. WESTON:** Hey! Before you hang out with Harriet, you should know that Frank Churchill and Jane Fairfax have been secretly engaged for a long time. Also, Frank's grumpy aunt died which means he can finally marry Jane. Okay, bye!

*(MRS. WESTON exits)*

**EMMA:** Oh great. Now I have to tell Harriet that I failed at match-making AGAIN.

*(HARRIET enters)*

**HARRIET:** Hey! What's up!

**EMMA:** Frank Churchill and Jane Fairfax are engaged.

**HARRIET:** Oh yeah! I just heard. I was backstage eavesdropping.

**EMMA:** And... you don't care?

**HARRIET:** Scoff. You do not think I care about Mr. Frank Churchill?

**EMMA:** Yeah huh! You basically told me you are in love with him.

**HARRIET:** No I didn't. I told you I am in love with Mr. Knightley!

**EMMA:** MR. KNIGHTLEY?!

**HARRIET:** I thought you knew. I talked about the great service he rendered me!

**EMMA:** I thought you meant the great service of Frank Churchill protecting you from the gypsies!

**HARRIET:** Oh yeah, that. No, I meant Mr. Knightley's coming and asking me to dance, when Mr. Elton would not stand up with me.

**EMMA:** Oh no. This is not good. *(to audience)* Because I just realized that I love Mr. Knightley.

**HARRIET:** This is awkward... I'm going to go look for a farmer. K bye!

*(ALL exit)*

*(enter EMMA; MR. KNIGHTLEY inconspicuously hiding behind a 'bush')*

**EMMA:** Harriet can't be in love with Mr. Knightley! Mr. Knightley must marry no one but myself!

*(MR. KNIGHTLEY pops out of a bush)*

**MR. KNIGHTLEY:** Emma!

**EMMA:** Ahhh! Why are you always hiding in bushes??

**MR. KNIGHTLEY:** The element of surprise. I love you! *(EMMA'S jaw drops)* Yes, you see, you understand my feelings.

**EMMA:** Duh! Because I love you too!

**MR. KNIGHTLEY:** High five! *(MR. KNIGHTLEY and EMMA jump and high five)* I almost forgot! Robert Martin and Harriet are engaged!

**EMMA:** Say whaaaaaaat?

*(enter ROBERT and HARRIET)*

**ROBERT & HARRIET:** We are!

**ROBERT:** YEEHAW!

**MR. KNIGHTLEY:** Yeah, sorry. I know you didn't want them to end up together.

**EMMA:** No, this is great! Especially because I failed every time I tried to set her up with someone!

**HARRIET:** Yes you did!

**MR. KNIGHTLEY:** Awesome! Well, let's all get married then!

*(ALL enter; COUPLES face each other)*

**COUPLES:** *(in unison)* I do! *(turn to audience)* The end!

# NOTES

# The 25-Minute or so
# EMMA
# for Kids

by Jane Austen
Creatively modified by
Amanda Thayer & Brendan P. Kelso
## 12-15 Actors

## CAST OF CHARACTERS:

**EMMA:** Wealthy, "match-maker" extraordinaire!

**MR. WOODHOUSE:** Emma's father

[1]**MR. KNIGHTLEY:** Wealthy; counsels Emma (whether she likes it or not!)

[2]**HARRIET SMITH:** Emma's friend, always falling in love

**MR. ELTON:** Vicar in Highbury

[3]**MRS. WESTON:** Previous governess of Emma (aka Miss Taylor)

**MR. WESTON:** Husband of Mrs. Weston

**MISS BATES:** Talkative, poor aunt of Jane Fairfax

**ROBERT MARTIN:** Farmer, totally in love with Harriet

[2]**ISABELLA KNIGHTLEY:** Older sister of Emma

[1]**JOHN KNIGHTLEY:** Husband of Isabella and brother of Mr. Knightley

**JANE FAIRFAX:** Educated and poor. Secret fiancé of Frank Churchill.

**FRANK CHURCHILL:** Son of Mr. Weston, raised by Churchill relatives.

**MRS. ELTON:** The new wife of Mr. Elton

[3]**SERVANT:** a servant

**The same actors can play the following parts:**
[1]MR. KNIGHTLEY and JOHN KNIGHTLEY
[2]HARRIET SMITH and ISABELLA KNIGHTLEY
[3]MR. WESTON and SERVANT

## ACT 1 SCENE 1

*(enter EMMA and MR. WOODHOUSE who is in despair)*

**MR. WOODHOUSE:** Poor Miss Taylor!— I wish she were here again. Emma, getting married is lame and makes everyone sad.

**EMMA:** I cannot agree with you, Papa. And now she has a house of her own!

**MR. WOODHOUSE:** Why would she want her own house?! Our house is three times as large! Downgrade much?

*(enter MR. KNIGHTLEY)*

**MR. KNIGHTLEY:** Congratulations! You must be so excited about Miss Taylor and Mr. Weston getting married.

**MR. WOODHOUSE:** Ugh. No.

**EMMA:** I'm happy. I was their match-maker, which is quite impressive, and you should be impressed.

*(MR. KNIGHTLEY is not impressed)*

**MR. KNIGHTLEY:** You did not. You made a lucky guess and that is all that can be said.

**EMMA:** Same thing! *(sticks tongue out)*

**MR. KNIGHTLEY:** Is not!

**EMMA:** Is too!

**MR. WOODHOUSE:** Please stop flirting. I'm trying to be sad.

*(EMMA and MR. KNIGHTLEY both look in opposite directions and start whistling awkwardly)*

**EMMA:** Sigh. But now I have no friends. No one in town is good enough to be my friend. You are probably my best friend now, Mr. Knightley. How depressing.

**MR. KNIGHTLEY:** Uhhhhhhhh..........

*(enter HARRIET)*

**HARRIET:** Wait! I'll be your best friend! My name is Harriet and I am young, naive, and have no family. You could probably take pity on me.

**EMMA:** I will take pity on you!

*(ALL exit)*

**ACT 1 SCENE 2**

*(enter EMMA and HARRIET; enter MR. KNIGHTLEY separately, he tries to blend in with the stage holding a 'bush')*

**EMMA:** Harriet, you are pretty and better than everyone else. Like me. With my help, you can become a real catch.

**HARRIET:** But I think I am already in love with the farmer, Robert Martin. I stayed with his sisters on their farm this summer.

**EMMA:** A farmer?!

**HARRIET:** Yes! Do you know him?

**EMMA:** Scoff. A young farmer, whether on horseback or on foot, is the very last sort of person to raise my curiosity. *(HARRIET looks dismayed)* Uhhhhh...what does he look like?

**HARRIET:** Oh! Not handsome. I thought him very plain at first, but I do not think him so plain now.

**EMMA:** Plain? He sounds... amazing. But you can't be in love with a farmer, especially a plain one. I'm going to set you up with hot Mr. Elton, the Vicar.

**HARRIET:** Yippee! I can't wait to go on a date with hot Mr. Elton.

**EMMA:** Hurray for my match-making powers!

*(enter ROBERT)*

**ROBERT:** Well howdy Harriet, I think you should marry me.

**HARRIET:** Ummm... hold that thought for a moment. *(turns to EMMA)* Robert Martin, THE FARMER, is proposing marriage to me. WHAT SHOULD I DO?! Emma, please help me!

**EMMA:** I really shouldn't tell you what to do... buuuut... ditch that guy and let me set you up with Mr. Elton.

**HARRIET:** You mean, HOT Mr. Elton?

**EMMA:** Exactly.

**HARRIET:** Okay, sounds good. *(turns back to ROBERT)* Mr. Martin, we need to talk.

*(they exit; EMMA does a victory dance)*

**MR. KNIGHTLEY:** Emma!

**EMMA:** *(startled)* Ahhhh!!!

**MR. KNIGHTLEY:** I just heard marvelous news! The farmer, Robert Martin, has proposed to Harriet.

**EMMA:** Mr. Knightley! Were you hiding in that bush??

**MR. KNIGHTLEY:** Uhhh no. Why would I do that? That would be weird.

**EMMA:** Oooooookayyyy.

*(awkward moment)*

**MR. KNIGHTLEY:** So, hurray for Robert Martin and Harriet!

**EMMA:** What? No, no, no! I just told Harriet to reject him! Isn't that great? Now she can marry a real gentleman! *(to audience)* Like hot Mr. Elton.

**MR. KNIGHTLEY:** Why would you do that?!

**EMMA:** *(sighs)* It is always incomprehensible to a man that a woman should ever refuse an offer of marriage. A man always imagines a woman to be ready for anybody who asks her.

**MR. KNIGHTLEY:** But no one else will ask her! She is the natural daughter of nobody knows whom. She is not a sensible girl and has been taught nothing useful.

**EMMA:** Ouch! She is still better than an ignorant farmer.

**MR. KNIGHTLEY:** Ignorant farmer?? Robert Martin is a respectable, intelligent gentleman-farmer!

**ROBERT:** *(offstage)* Yee-haw!

**EMMA:** You hear that?! Still a farmer! Ugh...you don't know anything! I think Harriet can do better than plain Robert Martin, so that is what will happen!

*(EMMA sticks tongue out at MR. KNIGHTLEY and exits; MR. KNIGHTLEY slaps hand against forehead and exits opposite)*

# ACT 1 SCENE 3

*(enter EMMA, HARRIET, and MR. ELTON)*

**EMMA:** Harriet, I would like to introduce you to Mr. Elton. Mr. Elton, this is Harriet. *(to audience)* Let the match-making skills commence!

**HARRIET:** Hello! *(gives subtle thumbs up to EMMA)*

**MR. ELTON:** Hi.

**EMMA:** I know what we should do! Did you ever have your likeness taken, Harriet?

**HARRIET:** Nope!

**MR. ELTON:** You should draw her, Emma! Let me entreat you to exercise so charming a talent in favor of your friend. You draw VERY well.

*(MR. ELTON picks up Emma's portfolio; drawings are all large pictures of stick figures)*

**EMMA:** I can't. I have given up drawing... Okay, you have convinced me! I will do it.

*(EMMA moves to an easel and begins drawing a stick figure of Harriet)*

**MR. ELTON:** Oh, Miss Woodhouse, it is brilliant! It looks just like her!

**EMMA:** Done!

*(EMMA turns the stick-figure picture around to show HARRIET)*

**HARRIET:** Gasp! Do you think it is a true likeness? It is way more beautiful than me. Emma, you are perfect at everything.

**EMMA:** I know.

**MR. ELTON:** I shall rush to London immediately to get it framed.

*(MR. ELTON grabs the picture and runs offstage)*

**EMMA:** He totally loves you.

**HARRIET:** You think?

*(EMMA nods; they exit high-fiving)*

# ACT 1 SCENE 4

*(enter EMMA and MR. ELTON from one direction; enter MRS. WESTON, JOHN, ISABELLA, and MR. WOODHOUSE from opposite)*

**EMMA:** It is such a bummer that Harriet is sick and couldn't make it to this Christmas party.

**MR. ELTON:** Yes. Poor Miss Smith. But, can I get YOU a drink, Miss Woodhouse? Do you want to hang out with me?

**EMMA:** Oh. Uhhhh. No, thank you.

**MR. ELTON:** What a wonderful dinner party this is! It is certainly a small party, but where small parties are select, they are perhaps the most agreeable of any.

**EMMA:** What?

**MR. ELTON:** It's easier to talk with people.

**EMMA:** Oh, yeah. Speaking of talking, I'm going to go talk to Mrs. Weston.

*(EMMA walks to MRS. WESTON)*

**EMMA:** *(to audience)* Mr. Elton must compose his joyous looks. Harriet seems quite forgotten in the expectation of a pleasant party.

**MRS. WESTON:** Hi, Emma!

**EMMA:** Hi, Mrs. Weston! I hear Frank Churchill, *(to audience)* the son Mr. Weston gave up when he was two, *(to Mrs. Weston)* is finally coming to visit.

**MRS. WESTON:** *(sighs)* I don't think he will really come.

**EMMA:** Yeah. Frank's grumpy aunt never lets him do anything. Hopefully, it works out!

**MRS. WESTON:** Hopefully! Also, I'm sorry Miss Smith is sick.

**EMMA:** I KNOW. Poor Harriet.

*(MR. ELTON pops out from behind EMMA and MRS. WESTON where he has been lurking)*

**MR. ELTON:** Poor Miss Smith! But, Mrs. Weston, you must promise to help me persuade Emma, I mean, Miss Woodhouse to stop visiting Miss Smith while she is sick. Miss Woodhouse is so scrupulous for others and yet so careless for herself. Is that fair, Mrs. Weston?

**MRS. WESTON:** Uh...

**JOHN:** *(to audience)* I am Mr. Knightley's brother and Emma's brother-in-law. *(to ISABELLA)* Isabella, we need to create a diversion!

**ISABELLA:** *(to audience)* I am Emma's older sister. *(to JOHN)* Gotcha!

**JOHN:** *(clearing throat)* It is snowing outside!

**ISABELLA:** Oh no! The children!

**JOHN:** We must go now, or we will never make it home!

**ISABELLA:** We must leave this party immediately!

**MR. WOODHOUSE:** We must leave now or we will all die in the snow!

*(JOHN and ISABELLA high-five; ALL exit except EMMA and MR. ELTON)*

**MR. ELTON:** Miss Woodhouse, I love you!

**EMMA:** Say whhhhaaaaattt??

**MR. ELTON:** Everything that I have said or done, for many weeks past, has been with the sole view of marking my admiration of yourself. I am sure you have seen and understood me.

**EMMA:** So you're saying you're not in love with Miss Smith? You know... Harriet?

**MR. ELTON:** Miss Smith?! I never thought of Miss Smith in the whole course of my existence. Who can think of Miss Smith when Miss Woodhouse is near?

**EMMA:** Very Shakespeare of you. Well, this stinks.

**MR. ELTON:** Stinks? That's a curious way to say you love me too.

**EMMA:** Ummm, yeah... not going to happen.

**MR. ELTON:** What?

**EMMA:** Let me see, how can I put this simply? .... I don't love you?

**MR. ELTON:** Ugh! Love? Fine then! Bye!

**EMMA:** Sorry. Geez. Bye.

*(ALL exit)*

*(enter EMMA, pacing)*

**EMMA:** Well, I messed up big time. I actually talked poor Harriet into being very much attached to this man. It was foolish, it was wrong, to take so active a part in bringing any two people together. I resolve to do such things no more.

*(EMMA sighs loudly; enter HARRIET)*

**HARRIET:** Hi! How was the party?

**EMMA:** This is awkward. Mr. Elton loves me. Not you.

*(HARRIET'S jaw drops, long silence)*

**EMMA:** Harriet, are you okay??

**HARRIET:** Obviously, I'm not good enough for him. I am sad.

*(HARRIET frowns exaggeratedly)*

**EMMA:** I will distract you with fun activities, so you don't think about him!

**HARRIET:** Should I think about the farmer?

**EMMA:** No.

**HARRIET:** Alright. Fun activities. That's fine I guess.

*(ALL exit)*

*(enter EMMA and HARRIET)*

**EMMA:** Harriet, let's visit Miss Bates. Miss Bates talks a LOT and is TOTALLY annoying, but it is our duty to be nice to her since she is poor.

*(EMMA and HARRIET walk around stage; enter MISS BATES)*

**MISS BATES:** Hello! It is so nice of you to come for a visit.

**EMMA:** Thank you for having us.

**MISS BATES:** Even though we are poor.

**EMMA:** Of course.

**MISS BATES:** So poor.

**EMMA:** Ahhh...

**MISS BATES:** Oh! Have I ever told you about my orphaned but well-educated niece, Jane Fairfax?

**EMMA:** Only literally every time I see you.

**MISS BATES:** She was raised by the Campbells' but now must forsake good society to become a governess.

**EMMA:** Oh.

**MISS BATES:** So sad.

**HARRIET:** Yes. So sad.

**MISS BATES:** Well, I received a letter stating she is coming to visit next week! Jane caught a bad cold last November. Her kind friends the Campbells think she had better come home and try an air that always agrees with her. Now I will read you her letter.

**EMMA:** *(to HARRIET)* Will this visit ever end?? *(to MISS BATES)* How wonderful for you that Jane is coming! But, I am afraid we must be running away. My father will be expecting us. Soooo... bye!

**MISS BATES:** But the letter...

**EMMA:** Next time!

*(EMMA grabs HARRIET'S hand and they rush off stage; MISS BATES exits opposite)*

*(enter EMMA opposite MISS BATES with JANE hiding behind)*

**MISS BATES:** Mr. Elton is getting married!

**EMMA:** Didn't I just see you??

**MISS BATES:** No. That was the other day. Plus, didn't you notice Jane is with me?

*(JANE sheepishly steps out from behind MISS BATES, eyes wide, staring at the floor)*

**EMMA:** Oh, hey, Jane. You look... tired?

*(JANE nods her head)*

**EMMA:** So. Wait. WHAT?! Who is Mr. Elton marrying?!

**MISS BATES:** A Miss Hawkins—that's all I know. A Miss Hawkins of Bath.

**EMMA:** Well, that was fast.

**MISS BATES:** Yes. But how exciting! Also, thank you for giving me that ham since I am poor. Bye!

*(MISS BATES exits; JANE quickly follows)*

**EMMA:** Ugh! Now I have to tell Harriet that Mr. Elton is engaged!

*(enter HARRIET)*

**EMMA:** *(to audience)* Let's get this over with. *(to HARRIET)* Mr. Elton is engaged!

**HARRIET:** Well that stinks! But guess what? I ran into Mr. Martin.

**EMMA:** The farmer? But...

**HARRIET:** *(continues over EMMA)* We talked and there was a sort of satisfaction in seeing him behave so pleasantly and so kindly. I think he might still be in love with me! *(to audience)* And I think I might still be in love with him!

**EMMA:** No more Robert Martin!

**HARRIET:** Whoops. Sorry. Please find someone else for me to love.

**EMMA:** On it.

*(ALL exit)*

# ACT 3 SCENE 1

*(Enter FRANK, MRS. WESTON, MISS BATES, JANE, and MR. KNIGHTLEY)*

**EMMA:** *(to audience)* We are at a dinner party at the Cole's. I'm better than them, but I came because my friends are here. Also, Frank Churchill finally came for a visit.

*(EMMA points to FRANK; he waves)*

**EMMA:** *(to FRANK)* Did you hear that Jane was sent a piano by a secret admirer?

**FRANK:** Oh REALLY?? I wonder who that could be from. *(winks at audience)*

**MRS. WESTON:** Pssst, Emma! Come here!

*(EMMA crosses to MRS. WESTON)*

**EMMA:** What's up?

**MRS. WESTON:** Did you know Mr. Knightley sent his own carriage to pick up Miss Bates and Jane Fairfax for the party tonight? I think he is the one who secretly sent her the piano!

**EMMA:** Well... he does like to do any thing really good-natured, useful, considerate, or benevolent.

**MRS. WESTON:** Now, I'm no expert at match-making like you, but what do you think of Mr. Knightley and Miss Fairfax being together?

**EMMA:** Mr. Knightley and Jane Fairfax! The imprudence of such a match. My dear Mrs. Weston, do not take to match-making. You do it very ill.

**MRS. WESTON:** I'm just saying. It could happen.

**EMMA:** Hmph! *(ALL exit)*

# ACT 3 SCENE 2

*(enter EMMA, FRANK, MR. WESTON, MRS. WESTON, and MISS BATES)*

**FRANK:** That dinner party was fun! We should throw our own ball!

**EMMA, MR. WESTON, MRS. WESTON, MISS BATES:** Yay!

*(SERVANT enters with a letter for FRANK)*

**FRANK:** *(opens and reads letter)* Shoot! I have to go back home and help my grumpy aunt! She is "sick" again. The ball must be postponed!

**EMMA, MR. WESTON, MRS. WESTON, MISS BATES:** Boooooooooo.

*(ALL exit except EMMA and FRANK)*

**FRANK:** See ya later, Emma! *(winks at her; exits)*

**EMMA:** Oh no! I think Frank Churchill might be in love with me! And worse, I think I might be in love with him!

*(EMMA paces around the room)*

**EMMA:** But I have sworn I will never get married! When he comes again, if his affection continue, I must be on my guard not to encourage it. *(EMMA sticks finger up like she has had an idea)* Maybe I can set Frank up with Harriet!

*(exits)*

*(enter EMMA, MRS. ELTON, MRS. WESTON, MISS BATES, JANE, and MR. KNIGHTLEY; ALL spread out and talk in pairs)*

**EMMA:** *(to audience)* The new Mrs. Elton has finally arrived. She is SUPER fancy and SUPER full of herself, but I have to throw her a dinner party to welcome her to our beautiful little town.

**MRS. ELTON:** What do you think of that poor Jane Fairfax? Can you believe she has to become a GOVERNESS?! That is, like, the worst job EVER!

**MRS. WESTON:** Cough! I'm standing right here!

**EMMA:** Mrs. Weston was my governess.

**MRS. ELTON:** Whoops. Sorry. Anyways, I am going to force Jane to be my friend and then I will find her a governess job in a big fancy house.

**EMMA:** That's nice of you... I guess.

**MRS. ELTON:** It is, isn't it? Hey! Miss Fairfax! Over here!

**JANE:** Hello.

**MRS. ELTON:** Jane, I am going to find you the perfect governess job. You have not seen so much of the world as I have. We must begin inquiring directly.

**JANE:** Excuse me, ma'am, but this is by no means my intention; I make no inquiry myself, and should be sorry to have any made by my friends.

**MRS. ELTON:** Fine. But I am going to keep bugging you about it!

*(enter MR. WESTON, hands a letter to MRS. WESTON)*

**MR. WESTON:** Sorry I'm late!

**MRS. WESTON:** *(opens and reads letter)* Hurray! Frank is coming to visit again!

*(ALL exit)*

# ACT 4 SCENE 1

*(enter EMMA, FRANK, MRS. WESTON, MR. WESTON, MISS BATES, JANE, MR. KNIGHTLEY, HARRIET, MR. ELTON, and MRS. ELTON; ALL spread out and talk in pairs)*

**EMMA:** *(to audience)* I have sworn to not let Frank fall in love with me, but I'm going to keep flirting with him. Because, well... it's fun!

**FRANK:** Will you dance with me? If you don't I might have to dance with Miss Fairfax. Ugh. *(winks at audience)*

**EMMA:** Of course! Everyone thinks we should dance together anyways!

*(EMMA and FRANK start to dance)*

**MR. ELTON:** Mrs. Weston, will you dance with me?

**MRS. WESTON:** No— I am no dancer. You should ask Harriet Smith!

**MR. ELTON:** *(cough-cough)* Uhhh... my dancing days are over, Mrs. Weston. You will excuse me.

*(HARRIET hears and is sad; MR. ELTON walks to talk to someone else; MR. KNIGHTLEY glares at him)*

**EMMA:** *(to MR. KNIGHTLEY)* What's with the evil eye?

**MR. KNIGHTLEY:** Watch this. *(crosses to HARRIET)* Miss Smith, will you dance with me?

**HARRIET:** Oh my goodness! Yes!

*(starts to dance; dance ends)*

**EMMA:** Mr. Knightley, thank you for dancing with Harriet.

**MR. KNIGHTLEY:** Mr. Elton stinks. Will you dance with me now?

**EMMA:** Indeed I will. You have shown that you can dance, and you know we are not really so much brother and sister as to make it at all improper.

*(EMMA and MR. KNIGHTLEY both wink at audience)*

*(ALL exit)*

*(enter EMMA and HARRIET)*

**HARRIET:** I am officially no longer in love with Mr. Elton. However, my life is still sad because now I am in love with someone infinitely better than him.

**EMMA:** I think I know who! *(to audience)* Frank Churchill. *(to Harriet)* The service he rendered you was enough to warm your heart. *(to audience)* He saved her from thieving gypsies.

**HARRIET:** Right?!

**EMMA:** But don't get carried away until you know whether he likes you back.

**HARRIET:** You always give the best advice.

**EMMA:** I know.

*(ALL exit)*

*(enter EMMA, FRANK, MRS. WESTON, MR. WESTON, MISS BATES, JANE, MR. KNIGHTLEY, HARRIET, MR. ELTON, and MRS. ELTON; ALL spread out and talk in pairs)*

**EMMA:** Ugh. This outing to Box Hill is a drag.

**FRANK:** I have an idea.

*(FRANK claps his hands three times)*

**FRANK:** Attention, everyone! Miss Woodhouse has asked me to lead a game where you all tell her clever things to impress her. Each of you must say one thing very clever, two things moderately clever, or three things very dull indeed.

**MISS BATES:** Oh! Very well, then I need not be uneasy. 'Three things very dull indeed.'

**EMMA:** *(laughing)* Yeah, but you can only say THREE things.

**MISS BATES:** *(frowning)* Ah! Yes, I see what she means. I talk too much. I must make myself very disagreeable. I am obviously a terrible person and no one should be my friend.

**JANE:** Let's go for a walk with Mrs. Elton.

**MISS BATES:** Yes. Good idea.

*(JANE, MRS. ELTON, and MISS BATES exit)*

**MR. KNIGHTLEY:** Emma! *(pause for ALL to awkwardly exit except MR. KNIGHTLEY and EMMA)* How could you be so unfeeling to Miss Bates? Did you forget that she is POOR?? We have to be nice to her! Poorly done, Emma... poorly done.

*(MR. KNIGHTLEY storms off stage)*

**EMMA:** *(to audience)* What is wrong with me? Why do I always think I am better than everyone? Mr. Knightley is always trying to help me be a better person, but I keep failing! I'll go to Miss Bates' house in the morning and apologize.

*(ALL exit)*

*(enter EMMA and MRS. WESTON)*

**MRS. WESTON:** Hey! Before you hang out with Harriet, you should know that Frank Churchill and Jane Fairfax have been secretly engaged for a long time. Also, Frank's grumpy aunt died which means he can finally marry Jane. Okay, bye!

*(MRS. WESTON exits)*

**EMMA:** Oh great. Now I have to tell Harriet that I failed at match-making AGAIN.

*(HARRIET enters)*

**HARRIET:** Hey! What's up!

**EMMA:** Frank Churchill and Jane Fairfax are engaged.

**HARRIET:** Oh yeah! I just heard. I was backstage eavesdropping.

**EMMA:** And... you don't care?

**HARRIET:** Scoff. You do not think I care about Mr. Frank Churchill?

**EMMA:** Yeah huh! You basically told me you are in love with him.

**HARRIET:** No I didn't. I told you I am in love with Mr. Knightley!

**EMMA:** MR. KNIGHTLEY?!

**HARRIET:** I thought you knew. I talked about the great service he rendered me!

**EMMA:** I thought you meant the great service of Frank Churchill protecting you from the gypsies!

**HARRIET:** Oh yeah, that. No, I meant Mr. Knightley's coming and asking me to dance, when Mr. Elton would not stand up with me.

**EMMA:** Oh no. This is not good. *(to audience)* Because I just realized that I love Mr. Knightley.

**HARRIET:** This is awkward... I'm going to go look for a farmer. K bye!

*(ALL exit)*

# ACT 4 SCENE 5

*(enter EMMA; MR. KNIGHTLEY inconspicuously hiding behind a 'bush')*

**EMMA:** Harriet can't be in love with Mr. Knightley! Mr. Knightley must marry no one but myself!

*(MR. KNIGHTLEY pops out of a bush)*

**MR. KNIGHTLEY:** Emma!

**EMMA:** Ahhh! Why are you always hiding in bushes??

**MR. KNIGHTLEY:** The element of surprise. I love you! *(EMMA'S jaw drops)* Yes, you see, you understand my feelings.

**EMMA:** Duh! Because I love you too!

**MR. KNIGHTLEY:** High five!

*(MR. KNIGHTLEY and EMMA jump and high five in the air)*

**MR. KNIGHTLEY:** I almost forgot! Robert Martin and Harriet are engaged!

**EMMA:** Say whaaaaaaat?

*(enter ROBERT and HARRIET)*

**ROBERT & HARRIET:** We are!

**ROBERT:** YEEHAW!

**MR. KNIGHTLEY:** Yeah, sorry. I know you didn't want them to end up together.

**EMMA:** No, this is great! Especially because I failed every time I tried to set her up with someone!

**HARRIET:** Yes you did!

**MR. KNIGHTLEY:** Awesome! Well, let's all get married then!

*(ALL enter; THE COUPLES stand facing each other)*

**COUPLES:** *(in unison)* I do! *(COUPLES turn to audience)* The end!

## THE END

# Author's note and Special Thanks

I never grew up a fan of Jane Austen's, or a fan or reading for that matter. However, over the years, I grew to love reading... but, Jane, not so much. However, thanks to my friends Khara and Amanda, I'm now a big Austen fan! Emma for Kids was a special play to create, as Amanda gave it to me as a way to say, "see, I can write with your humor!" At that time, I wasn't in to it, nor did I even ask for it. I found it sitting in my archived emails a few months back and was surprised by how well it read and how funny it was. Knowing how great Jane is now and reading this, I knew it was the right time to release this. So, thank you Amanda and enjoy!

First, a big shout out to Mr. Rod's 2021-2022 6th Grade Theatre class at Pecan Trail Intermediate as well as Mr Murray's Theatre Class at Crespo Elementary in the Houston Independent School District. These two teachers took this play and workshopped in with their classes. I always love the creative ideas the kids bring!

And as always, a big thank you to all our beta readers who are ALWAYS improving our scripts! Khara C. Barnhart, Isidro, Pamela, Kenny, Melisa, Royce, and Catherine. What a great list! Our books are not what their potential is, without our Betas!!!

-Brendan

# Sneak Peeks at other
# Playing With Plays books:

# The Tempest for Kids

**PROSPERO:** Hast thou, spirit, performed to point the tempest that I bade thee?

**ARIEL:** What? Was that English?

**PROSPERO:** *(Frustrated)* Did you make the storm hit the ship?

**ARIEL:** Why didn't you say that in the first place? Oh yeah! I rocked that ship! They didn't know what hit them.

**PROSPERO:** Why, that's my spirit! But are they, Ariel, safe?

**ARIEL:** Not a hair perished.

**PROSPERO:** Woo-hoo! All right. We've got more work to do.

**ARIEL:** Wait a minute. You're still going to free me, right, Master?

**PROSPERO:** Oh, I see. Is it sooooo terrible working for me? Huh? Remember when I saved you from that witch? Do you? Remember when that blue-eyed hag locked you up and left you for dead? Who saved you? Me, that's who!

**ARIEL:** I thank thee, master.

**PROSPERO:** I will free you in two days, okay? Sheesh. Patience is a virtue, or haven't you heard. Right. Where was I? Oh yeah... I need you to disguise yourself like a sea nymph and then... *(PROSPERO whispers something in ARIEL'S ear)* Got it?

**ARIEL:** Got it. *(ARIEL exits)*

**PROSPERO:** *(to MIRANDA)* Awake, dear heart, awake!

*(MIRANDA yawns loudly)*

**PROSPERO:** Shake it off. Come on. We'll visit Caliban, my slave.

**MIRANDA:** The witch's son? You mean the MONSTER! He's creepy and stinky!!!

**PROSPERO:** Mysterious and sneaky,

**MIRANDA:** Altogether freaky,

**MIRANDA & PROSPERO:** He's Caliban the slave!!! *(snap, snap!)*

**PROSPERO:** *(Calls offstage)* What, ho! Slave! Caliban!

*(enter CALIBAN)*

**CALIBAN:** Oh, look it's the island stealers! This is my home! My mother, the witch, left it to me and now you treat me like dirt.

**MIRANDA:** Oh boo-hoo! I used to feel sorry for you, I even taught you our language, but you tried to hurt me so now we have to lock you in that cave.

**CALIBAN:** I wish I had never learned your language!

**PROSPERO:** Go get us wood! If you don't, I'll rack thee with old cramps, and fill all thy bones with aches!

**CALIBAN:** *(to AUDIENCE)* He's so mean to me! But I have to do what he says. ANNOYING! *(exit CALIBAN)*

*(enter FERDINAND led by "invisible" ARIEL)*

**ARIEL:** *(Singing)* Who let the dogs out?! Woof, woof, woof!! *(Spookily)* The watchdogs bark; bow-wow, bow-wow!

**FERDINAND:** *(Dancing across stage)* Where should this music be? Where is it taking me! What's going on?

# Two Gentlemen of Verona for Kids

**ANTONIO**: It's not nothing.

**PROTEUS**: Ahhhhh......It's a letter from Valentine, telling me what a great time he's having in Milan, yeah... that's what it says!

**ANTONIO**: Awesome! Glad to hear it! Because, you leave tomorrow to join Valentine in Milan.

**PROTEUS**: What!? Dad! No way! I don't want... I mean, I need some time. I've got some things to do.

**ANTONIO**: Like what?

**PROTEUS**: You know...things! Important things! And stuff! Lots of stuff!

**ANTONIO**: No more excuses! Go pack your bag. *(ANTONIO begins to exit)*

**PROTEUS**: Fie!

**ANTONIO**: What was that?

**PROTEUS**: Fiiii.......ne with me, Pops! *(ANTONIO exits)* I was afraid to show my father Julia's letter, lest he should take exceptions to my love; and my own lie of an excuse made it easier for him to send me away.

**ANTONIO**: *(Offstage)* Proteus! Get a move on!!

**PROTEUS**: Fie!!!

*(exit)*

## ACT 2 SCENE 1

*(enter VALENTINE and SPEED following)*

**VALENTINE**: Ah, Silvia, Silvia! *(heavy sighs)*

**SPEED**: *(mocking)* Madam Silvia! Madam Silvia! Gag me.

**VALENTINE**: Knock it off! You don't know her.

**SPEED**: Do too. She's the one that you can't stop staring at. Makes me wanna barf.

**VALENTINE**: I do not stare!

**SPEED**: You do. AND you keep singing that silly love song. *(sing INSERT SAPPY LOVE SONG)* You used to be so much fun.

**VALENTINE**: Huh? *(heavy sigh, starts humming SAME LOVE SONG)*

**SPEED**: Never mind.

**VALENTINE**: I have loved her ever since I saw her. Here she comes!

**SPEED**: Great. *(to audience)* Watch him turn into a fool.

*(enter SILVIA)*

**VALENTINE**: Hey, Silvia.

**SILVIA**: Hey, Valentine. What's goin' on?

**VALENTINE**: Nothin'. What's goin' on with you?

**SILVIA**: Nothin'.

*(pause)*

**VALENTINE**: What are you doing later?

**SILVIA**: Not sure. Prob-ly nothin'. You?

**VALENTINE**: Me neither. Nothin'.

**SILVIA**: Yea?

**VALENTINE**: Probably.

SPEED: *(to audience)* Kill me now.

SILVIA: Well, I guess I better go.

VALENTINE: Oh, okay! See ya'..

*(pause)*

SILVIA: See ya' later maybe?

VALENTINE: Oh, yea! Maybe! Yea! Okay!

SILVIA: Bye.

VALENTINE: Bye!

*(exit SILVIA)*

SPEED: *(aside)* Wow. *(to VALENTINE)* Dude, what the heck was that?

VALENTINE: I think she has a boyfriend. I can tell.

SPEED: Dude! She is so into you! How could you not see that?

VALENTINE: Do you think?

SPEED: Come on. We'll talk it through over dinner. *(to audience)* Fool. Am I right?

*(exit)*

     

Sneak peek of

# Christmas Carol
# for Kids

*(enter GHOST PRESENT wearing a robe and holding a turkey leg and a goblet)*

**GHOST PRESENT:** Wake up, Scrooge! I am the Ghost of Christmas Present. Look upon me!

**SCROOGE:** I'm looking. Not that impressed. But let's get on with it.

**GHOST PRESENT:** Touch my robe! *(SCROOGE touches GHOST PRESENT's robe. Pause. They look at each other)* Er...it must be broken. Guess we walk. Come on. *(they begin walking downstage)*

**SCROOGE:** Where are we going?

**GHOST PRESENT:** Your employee, Bob Cratchit's house. Oh look, here we are.

*(enter BOB, MRS. CRATCHIT, MARTHA CRATCHIT, and TINY TIM, who has a crutch in one hand; they are all holding bowls)*

**BOB:** *(to audience)* Hi, we're the Cratchit family. We are a REALLY happy family!

**MRS. CRATCHIT:** *(to audience)* Yes, but we're REALLY poor, too. Thanks to HIS boss! *(pointing at BOB)*

**MARTHA:** *(to audience)* Yeah, as you can see our bowls are empty. *(shows empty bowl)* We practically survive off air.

**TINY TIM:** *(to audience)* But we're happy!

**MRS. CRATCHIT:** *(to audience; overly sappy)* Because we have each other.

**TINY TIM:** And love!

**SCROOGE:** *(to GHOST PRESENT)* Seriously, are they for real?

**GHOST PRESENT:** Yep! Adorable, isn't it?

**BOB:** A merry Christmas to us all.

**TINY TIM:** God bless us every one!

**SCROOGE:** Spirit, tell me if Tiny Tim will live.

**GHOST PRESENT:** *(puts hands to head as if looking into the future)* Ooooo, not so good....I see a vacant seat in the poor chimney corner, and a crutch without an owner. If SOMEBODY doesn't change SOMETHING, the child will die.

**SCROOGE:** No, no! Say he will be spared.

**GHOST PRESENT:** Nope, can't do that, sorry. Unless SOMEONE decides to change...hint, hint.

**BOB:** A Christmas toast to my boss, Mr. Scrooge! The founder of the feast!

**MRS. CRATCHIT:** *(angrily)* Oh sure, Mr. Scrooge! If he were here I'd give him a piece of my mind to feast upon. What an odious, stingy, hard, unfeeling man!

**BOB:** Dear, it's Christmas day. He's not THAT bad. *(Pause)* He's just... THAT sad. *(BOB holds up his bowl)* Come on, kids, to Scrooge! He probably needs it more than us!

**MARTHA & TINY TIM:** *(holding up their bowls)* To Scrooge!

**MRS. CRATCHIT:** *(muttering)* Thanks for nothing.

**BOB:** That's not nice.

**MARTHA:** And we Cratchits are ALWAYS nice. Read

the book, Mom.

**MRS. CRATCHIT:** Sorry.

*(the CRATCHIT FAMILY exits)*

**SCROOGE:** She called me odious! Do I really smell that bad?

**GHOST PRESENT:** Odious doesn't mean you stink. Although in this case you do... According to the dictionary, odious means "unequivocally detestable." I mean, you are a toad sometimes Mr. Scrooge.

**SCROOGE:** Wow... that's kind of ... mean.

# Oliver Twist
# for Kids

*(enter FAGIN, SIKES, DODGER and NANCY)*

**DODGER:** So that Oliver kid got caught by the police.

**FAGIN:** He could tell them all our secrets and get us in trouble; we've got to find him. Like, in the next 30 seconds or so.

**SIKES:** Send Nancy. She's good at getting information quick.

**NANCY:** Nope. Don't wanna go, Sikes. I like the kid.

**SIKES:** She'll go, Fagin.

**NANCY:** No, she won't, Fagin.

**SIKES:** Yes, she will, Fagin.

**NANCY:** Fine! Grrrrr....

*(NANCY sticks out her tongue at SIKES and storms offstage, then immediately returns)*

**NANCY:** Okay, I checked with my sources and, some gentleman took him home to take care of him.

*(NANCY, DODGER and SIKES stare at FAGIN waiting for direction)*

**FAGIN:** Where?

**NANCY:** I don't know.

**FAGIN:** WHAT!?!? *(waiting)* Well don't just stand there, GO FIND HIM! *(to audience)* Can't find any good help these days!

*(all run offstage, bumping into each other in their haste)*

**ACT 2 SCENE 2**

*(enter OLIVER)*

**OLIVER:** *(to audience)* I'm out running an errand for Mr. Brownlow to prove that I'm a trustworthy boy. I can't keep hanging out with thieves, right?

*(enter NANCY, who runs over to OLIVER and grabs him; SIKES, FAGIN, and DODGER enter shortly after and follow NANCY)*

**NANCY:** Oh my dear brother! I've found him! Oh! Oliver! Oliver!

**OLIVER:** What!?!? I don't have a sister!

**NANCY:** You do now, kid. Let's go. *(she drags OLIVER to FAGIN)*

**FAGIN:** Dodger, take Oliver and lock him up.

**DODGER:** *(to OLIVER)* Sorry, dude. *(DODGER and OLIVER start to exit)*

**OLIVER:** Aw, man! Seriously? I just found a good home...

**NANCY:** Don't be too mean to him, Fagin.

**OLIVER:** *(as he's exiting)* Yeah, don't be too mean to me, Fagin!

**SIKES:** *(mimicking NANCY)* Don't be mean, Fagin. Wah, wah, wah. Look, I need Oliver to help me rob a house, okay? He is just the size I want to fit through the window. All sneaky ninja like.

# Macbeth for Kids

## ACT 2 SCENE 1

*(DUNCAN runs on stage and dies with a dagger stuck in him, MACBETH drags his body off and then returns with the bloody dagger. LADY MACBETH enters)*

**LADY MACBETH:** Did you do it?

**MACBETH:** *(clueless)* Do what?

**LADY MACBETH:** KILL HIM!

**MACBETH:** Oh yeah, all done. I have done the deed.

**LADY MACBETH:** *(pointing at the dagger)* What is that?

**MACBETH:** What?

**LADY MACBETH:** Why do you still have the bloody dagger with you?

**MACBETH:** Ummmmm, I don't know.

**LADY MACBETH:** Well go put it back!

**MACBETH:** NO! I'll go no more! I'm scared of the dark, and there is a dead body in there. I am afraid to think what I have done.

**LADY MACBETH:** Man you are a wimp, give me the dagger. *(LADY MACBETH takes the dagger, exits, and returns)*

**LADY MACBETH:** All done.

*(there is a loud knock at the door)*

**LADY MACBETH:** It's 2am! This really is not a good time for more visitors. *(goes to the door)* Who is it? *(opens door)*

**MACDUFF**: It is Macduff. I am here to see the king.

**MACBETH**: He is sleeping in there.

*(MACDUFF exits while MACBETH and LADY MACBETH look at each other)*

**MACDUFF**: *(offstage scream)* AGHHHHHHHHHHH – He's dead, he's dead!!! *(MACDUFF enters)*

**MACBETH**: Who?

**MACDUFF**: Who do you think? *(they both scream)*

**BANQUO**: *(BANQUO, MALCOLM, and DONALBAIN enter)* What happened, can't someone get a good night sleep around here?

**MACDUFF**: The king has been murdered.

**MALCOLM & DONALBAIN**: Aghhhhhhhh!!!!!!!!!

**DONALBAIN**: We must be next.

**MALCOLM**: Let's get out of here.

**DONALBAIN**: I'm heading to Ireland.

**MALCOLM**: I'm off to England. *(MALCOLM and DONALBAIN exit)*

**MACDUFF**: Well, since there is no one left to be King, why don't you do it Mac?

**LADY MACBETH & MACBETH**: Okay. *(LADY MACBETH, MACBETH and MACDUFF exit)*

**BANQUO**: *(to audience)* I fear, thou play'dst most foully for't. *(MACBETH returns)*

**MACBETH**: Bank, what are you thinking over there?

**BANQUO**: Oh, nothing. *(said with a big fake smile)* Gotta go! See ya! *(BANQUO exits)*

# ABOUT THE AUTHORS

**AMANDA THAYER** loves books more than most things (excepting maybe her husband and children). She has a B.A. in English and a Master of Library Studies from the University of North Carolina at Greensboro. She is also an actress and dramaturg, having worked with SLO Repertory Theatre, The Great American Melodrama, and PCPA. Amanda grew up performing and understands the importance of youth arts programs. Amanda likes to laugh and she hopes you do too!

**BRENDAN P. KELSO** came to writing modified Shakespeare scripts when he was taking time off from work to be at home with his newly born son. "It just grew from there". Within months, he was being asked to offer classes in various locations and acting organizations along the Central Coast of California. Originally employed as an engineer, Brendan never thought about writing. However, his unique personality, humor, and love for engaging the kids with The Bard has led him to leave the engineering world and pursue writing as a new adventure in life! He has always believed, "the best way to learn is to have fun!" Brendan makes his home on the Central Coast of California and loves to spend time with his wife and kids.

# CAST AUTOGRAPHS